INSIDE MLS

SPORTING KANSAS CITY

BY JONATHAN AVISE

SportsZone

An Imprint of Abdo Publishing
abdobooks.com

abdobooks.com

Published by Abdo Publishing, a division of ABDO, PO Box 398166, Minneapolis, Minnesota 55439. Copyright © 2022 by Abdo Consulting Group, Inc. International copyrights reserved in all countries. No part of this book may be reproduced in any form without written permission from the publisher. SportsZone™ is a trademark and logo of Abdo Publishing.

Printed in the United States of America, North Mankato, Minnesota
052021
092021

THIS BOOK CONTAINS RECYCLED MATERIALS

Cover Photo: Scott Winters/Icon Sportswire/AP Images
Interior Photos: Colin E. Braley/AP Images, 4–5, 7, 9; Jamie Squire/Getty Images Sport/Getty Images, 10; AP Images, 12–13; Chris Martinez/AP Images, 15; Ed Zurga/AP Images, 16; Darren Carroll/Sports Illustrated/Set Number: X61560 TK3 R4 F8/Getty Images, 19; Charlie Riedel/AP Images, 21; Kyle Ross/Icon Sportswire/AP Images, 22–23; Scott Indermaur/MLS/Allsport/Getty Images Sport, 25; Nick Wass/AP Images, 27; Elsa/Getty Images Sport/Getty Images, 28; George Holland/Cal Sport Media/AP Images, 30; Nick Tre. Smith/Icon Sportswire/AP Images, 33; Doug Pensinger/Allsport/Getty Images Sport/Getty Images, 35; Mario Tama/AFP/Getty Images, 36; Mike Ransdell/The Kansas City Star/AP Images, 38; Kyle Rivas/Cal Sport Media/AP Images, 40; Orlin Wagner/AP Images, 43

Editor: Patrick Donnelly
Series Designer: Dan Peluso

Library of Congress Control Number: 2019954424

Publisher's Cataloging-in-Publication Data
Names: Avise, Jonathan, author.
Title: Sporting Kansas City / by Jonathan Avise
Description: Minneapolis, Minnesota : Abdo Publishing, 2022 | Series: Inside MLS | Includes online resources and index.
Identifiers: ISBN 9781532192630 (lib. bdg.) | ISBN 9781644945711 (pbk.) | ISBN 9781098210533 (ebook)
Subjects: LCSH: Sporting Kansas City (Soccer team)--Juvenile literature. | Soccer teams--Juvenile literature. | Professional sports franchises--Juvenile literature. | Sports Teams--Juvenile literature.
Classification: DDC 796.334--dc23

TABLE OF CONTENTS

CHAPTER 1
SPORTING TAKES THE CROWN.................... 4

CHAPTER 2
FROM SPURS TO SPORTING...... 12

CHAPTER 3
KC LEGENDS.................... 24

CHAPTER 4
MEMORABLE MOMENTS.......... 34

TIMELINE	44
TEAM FACTS	45
GLOSSARY	46
MORE INFORMATION	47
ONLINE RESOURCES	47
INDEX	48
ABOUT THE AUTHOR	48

CHAPTER 1

SPORTING TAKES
THE CROWN

On an icy December afternoon in 2013, Sporting KC did what was once unthinkable. It helped confirm that its hometown—where American football had long been king—had become a true soccer hotbed.

The 2013 Major League Soccer (MLS) season had already been a big one for the club. In July Kansas City had hosted the league's All-Star game in its two-year-old stadium built specifically for soccer. Now, the team was trying to win its second league championship.

The team had come a long way from just a few seasons earlier. Known first as the Wiz and then as the Wizards, the club had success in MLS' early years. The Wizards even won a league title in 2000. But those glory days felt long ago.

Sporting KC fans bundled up for the cold as they cheered for their team in the 2013 MLS Cup.

The club had often played before some of the smallest crowds in the league, first at a cavernous football stadium and then at a minor league baseball park.

But with a move into a brand-new, soccer-specific stadium in 2011, things began to change. The club, newly renamed Sporting KC—often abbreviated as Sporting or SKC—made the first of eight straight playoff appearances that year. By 2013 the team was back among the league's elite. Fans packed into the team's new stadium as Kansas City went 17–10–7 to reach the playoffs for the third year in a row. Then it made a run all the way to the MLS Cup.

On a day featuring rugged weather more suited to American football, Sporting hosted the MLS Cup final against Real Salt Lake. Fans bundled up and players struggled through 20-degree temperatures during one of the coldest MLS games ever played. A full stadium stood, sang, and cheered despite the cold. But time began to run out on Sporting KC's championship dreams. After a scoreless first half, Real Salt Lake took the lead in the 52nd minute on a goal by Álvaro Saborío.

SKC then fought off attack after attack to prevent the deficit from growing. Two Salt Lake shots bounded off the post, both

Real Salt Lake midfielder Ned Grabavoy, *left*, and Sporting Kansas City midfielder Benny Feilhaber display the intensity of the MLS Cup action.

nearly putting the title out of reach. But Sporting, led by US national team players Graham Zusi and Matt Besler, held on.

Then, with less than 15 minutes left in the game, SKC found new life. The team earned a corner kick. It would be taken right

STARS VISIT KC

The 2013 MLS Cup final wasn't the only glamorous match Sporting Park hosted in 2013. In July the stadium was the site of the 2013 MLS All-Star Game. A sellout crowd of 21,175 saw a team of MLS stars lose to Italian club AS Roma 3–1. The MLS team included Sporting KC players Matt Besler, Aurélien Collin, and Graham Zusi. The All-Stars were managed by SKC head coach Peter Vermes.

in front of The Cauldron, where Sporting's most rabid fans gather to cheer for the team.

Zusi's perfectly placed ball arced high into the air in front of the Salt Lake goal. Defender Aurélien Collin leapt high above every other player in the crowded penalty area. His forehead met the ball and his powerful header sent it into the bottom corner of the net. Kansas City was still alive. The game was tied again, 1–1.

After 90 minutes of soccer on a frozen field, the teams still remained level. Another 30 minutes of extra time couldn't separate them either. The MLS Cup would be decided by a penalty kick shootout.

SUDDEN DEATH DECIDES IT

Each team had five shooters to break the deadlock. Even that wasn't enough to separate these two teams. After five kicks each, the score was still tied. Now, the shootout went into

Sporting KC goalkeeper Jimmy Nielsen makes a diving save to keep his team alive during the shootout.

sudden death. After six, seven, eight, and then nine shooters the score remained even.

   Then, Kansas City's Collin came up big again. Never before in his career had Sporting's No. 78 taken a penalty kick. But with the pressure of a league championship on the line, the unlikely hero calmly thumped his penalty kick past the goalkeeper to give Kansas City a 7-6 lead.

Aurélien Collin was the unlikely hero of the 2013 MLS Cup.

"Nobody wants to see a game like that decided on penalty kicks," Collin said after the match. "Except tonight."

Now, Sporting goalkeeper Jimmy Nielsen stood on his goal line, waiting for history to unfold. Nielsen had saved one sudden-death penalty kick already to keep Sporting alive. Twelve yards away, Real Salt Lake's Lovel Palmer stood ready to take his team's kick. The MLS Cup was on the line. Palmer had to score, or the title would go to Sporting KC.

It had been a hard-fought game in the bitter cold. The breath of 22 exhausted players hung in the wintry Kansas City air. A stadium full of fans wearing Sporting KC's blue were on their feet.

Palmer stepped up to the penalty spot. He swung his right foot hard at the ball. On the goal line, Nielsen dove to his left. He had guessed wrong. The ball headed straight at the middle of the goal. But to Kansas City's delight, the Salt Lake defender's shot was too high. It clanged off the crossbar and the game—finally—was over.

Sporting Kansas City were champions of Major League Soccer for the first time in 13 years. They had a new identity and a new stadium packed with their fans. Now they had a second league title.

CHAPTER 2

FROM SPURS TO SPORTING

Sporting KC was not the Kansas City metro area's first soccer champion. The short-lived Kansas City Spurs hold that honor. Professional soccer in Kansas City got its start in 1968 when the red-clad Spurs took the field in the North American Soccer League (NASL).

The Spurs spent three seasons in Kansas City after moving from Chicago, where they played in a different league. They had a short but successful stay in Kansas City. In their first two years the Spurs took the field at Municipal Stadium, which also housed the city's pro baseball and football teams, the Royals and Chiefs. The Spurs, fielding international players such as Ireland's Joe Haverty and Brazil's Iris DeBrito, dazzled their new home fans.

Tony Galvin (22) of the St. Louis Steamers battles two Kansas City Comets for the ball in a 1981 Major Indoor Soccer League match. The Comets played to large crowds in the 1980s in Kansas City.

KANSAS CITY COMETS

Kansas City wasn't completely without professional soccer after the NASL's Spurs left town. The Comets played in the Major Indoor Soccer League from 1981 to 1991. Indoor soccer is played on a small field inside a hockey rink. It excited local soccer fans. The Comets drew an average of 11,500 fans per game during the 1981–82 season. That was more than the local National Basketball Association (NBA) team, the Kansas City Kings, drew that season.

And they were successful, too. In their first season, the Spurs reached the conference finals. A year later, they topped that feat. In 1969 the Spurs won the NASL championship, beating the Baltimore Bays on the final day of the season to win the crown. It marked the city's first major league sports championship, coming just months before the Chiefs' Super Bowl victory.

That was the high point of the team's brief stay. Following the 1970 season, amid financial turmoil throughout the league, the Spurs folded.

WELCOMING THE WIZ

Twenty-five years later, Kansas City soccer fans got another chance to celebrate. Outdoor professional men's soccer was coming back to town.

Major League Soccer was founded as part of an even bigger event. In 1994 more than 3.5 million fans attended World Cup

Mo Johnston of the Wiz, *left*, leaps high for a header against the Galaxy in a 1996 match at the Rose Bowl.

games across the United States. As part of the bid to host the event, US Soccer had pledged to launch a new professional men's soccer league. In 1995 Kansas City was awarded one of 10 original MLS teams. And in 1996 that new team, the Kansas City Wiz, took the field.

Preki, *right*, was Kansas City's first star player.

The team hit the ground running on April 13, 1996. Before 21,141 fans, the Wiz won the first game in their history 3–0 over the Colorado Rapids. The club's first goal came from forward Vitalis "Digital" Takawira in the 71st minute. Six minutes later, Frank Klopas, who had been the team's second player signed, netted Kansas City's second goal. Takawira then added his second goal of the game to wrap up the win.

Led by their star Preki and his 18 goals that season, the Wiz finished third in the new MLS Western Conference. Their 17–15 record included five shootout victories, as MLS did not allow ties in its early years. A close loss in the conference finals, however, ended the team's first season.

Year two brought a new name—the Wiz were now called the Wizards. It also brought more success. The team's 21–11 record tied them with DC United of the Eastern Conference for the best record in the league. But despite their status as the best in the West, the Wizards' season ended in disappointment. Colorado pulled off an upset in the conference semifinals.

Kansas City's star again was Preki. The Yugoslavian-born midfielder was named the 1997 MLS Most Valuable Player (MVP). He scored 12 goals that season, good for fourth in the league. And he would represent the United States at the 1998 World Cup a year later.

WINNING WIZARDS

After falling short in the playoffs during their first two seasons, the Wizards missed the postseason entirely the next two years.

Kansas City finally had its big breakthrough in 2000. Behind important offseason signings such as American defender Peter Vermes and Danish forward Miklos Molnar, the team began the season 10–0–2. The Wizards finished atop the league during the regular season. For that achievement, they earned their first trophy. The MLS Supporters' Shield goes to the team with the best regular-season record.

This time Kansas City would not trip up in the postseason. The team advanced easily into the semifinals. There a goal by Molnar in extra time put the Wizards into their first MLS Cup, the league's championship game.

The hero of Kansas City's first MLS Cup wasn't one of its high-scoring forwards or midfielders. It was goalkeeper Tony Meola. On a Sunday afternoon in October at Washington, DC's RFK Stadium, Meola stopped shot after shot from the Chicago Fire. The US World Cup veteran made 10 saves in all, including a series of diving stops late in the game. Thanks to Meola, the Wizards' 11th-minute goal—again by Molnar— was good enough for the 1–0 win. Kansas City had a soccer champion again.

The Wizards followed that league title with another important trophy in 2004. The Lamar Hunt US Open Cup,

Goalkeeper Tony Meola was the defensive leader of the 2000 MLS Cup–winning Wizards.

named for the founder and owner of Kansas City's franchise, is the oldest soccer competition in the United States. The tournament pits teams from all levels of US soccer against one another, from the best of MLS to teams that field part-time players.

Kansas City survived the knockout competition to reach the final for the first time. And again, they met the Fire with a trophy on the line. Igor Simutenkov's golden goal in extra time gave the Wizards a 1–0 win and their first US Open Cup.

Later that season, the team reached another MLS Cup final. This time, however, the Wizards fell short in a 3–2 loss to DC United.

FINDING A NEW IDENTITY

Despite that early success on the field, Kansas City faced difficulties. Attendance was low, with the team playing in front of a sea of empty seats at Arrowhead Stadium.

In 2005 Hunt began looking to sell the franchise. Rumors the team would be relocated to another city kept local fans on edge. Fans, elected officials, and business leaders worked to keep the Wizards in Kansas City.

Sporting Kansas City moved into a new soccer-only stadium in 2011.

Big changes began to take place. A new ownership group took over in 2006. The club returned to the playoffs in 2007. The next year, they moved to a new stadium. The Wizards left the American football stadium they had called home since 1996. A cozy minor league baseball stadium was their home until 2011, when even more dramatic changes occurred.

The team moved into a gleaming new 18,467-seat stadium built solely for soccer. It also adopted a new name: Sporting Kansas City. Sellout crowds squeezed into Kansas City's new stadium, and the team began piling up wins.

Sporting KC players celebrate their 2015 US Open Cup championship.

Under coach Peter Vermes, who came aboard in 2009, SKC established itself as a regular contender on the field. After a two-season absence, the team returned to the playoffs in 2011 and 2012. But it came up short both years, losing two playoff heartbreakers to the Houston Dynamo.

That changed in 2013. Sporting was led by hometown defender Matt Besler, midfielder Graham Zusi, and high-scoring forward Dom Dwyer. They got revenge by beating Houston

in the conference finals on their way to the MLS Cup. Before another sold-out home crowd on a frigid day, Kansas City captured its second league title thanks to another dramatic penalty shootout victory over Real Salt Lake.

That was just the start. US Open Cup victories followed in 2015 and 2017, giving Sporting KC four trophies in six years. Before a packed stadium, a team that had cycled through three home stadiums and two team names had found its identity. Sporting Kansas City were winners.

CHAPTER 3

KC LEGENDS

He was born Predrag Radosavljević on June 24, 1963, in Belgrade, Yugoslavia. But to Kansas City soccer fans, the city's first MLS-era star will always be known by a much shorter name: Preki.

The attacking midfielder wowed fans and overwhelmed opponents. Preki spent all but one season of his 10-year MLS career with the Wizards. In that time, his 79 career goals and 112 assists made him the league's all-time leading scorer. He led an attack that also included high-scoring midfielder Chris Klein to the 2000 MLS Cup.

Preki twice won the MLS Most Valuable Player (MVP) Award, in 1997 and again in 2003. His second MVP season came when he was 40 years old, an age when many players

Preki helped fill the trophy case in the early days of the Wizards.

have long since retired. When he did finally leave the game, Preki was made a member of the US National Soccer Hall of Fame.

WIZARDS' WALL

In soccer, the glory often goes to goal-scorers like Preki and Chris Klein. The latter, a St. Louis native, scored 43 goals and added 54 assists over 235 games with the Wizards from 1998 to 2005. All of those goals don't account for much if you can't stop the other team from scoring, though. Thankfully for the Wizards, they had Tony Meola.

Meola was a fixture on the US men's national team for more than a decade. He started in goal for the US team during the 1990 and 1994 World Cups and was an alternate on the 2002 squad.

The New Jersey native joined the Wizards before the 1999 season. A year later, he had one of the best seasons an MLS keeper has ever had. Meola swept up awards at every turn in 2000. He set a league record with 16 shutouts that season. He was named league MVP and Goalkeeper of the Year during the regular season. And Meola's 10 saves in the MLS Cup earned him the game's MVP award as Kansas City won its first

Tony Meola came up huge in the net for the Wizards.

Peter Vermes went from stout defender to venerable coach in Kansas City.

league title. In six seasons with the Wizards, Meola managed 37 regular-season shutouts.

BACKLINE TO SIDELINE

Even the best goalkeepers won't keep the ball out of the net without plenty of help. A strong defense in front of them limits their opponent's chance to score.

Defender Peter Vermes was a huge part of making the Wizards' 2000 defense the toughest in MLS. With Meola in net and Vermes in the backline, Kansas City allowed the fewest number of goals in the league.

It's possible no one has had a bigger impact on Kansas City's MLS history than Vermes. He arrived as a tough and talented veteran defender before that 2000 season. His presence that season played a huge role in turning the Wizards into MLS champions.

Vermes retired in 2002, then joined the KC coaching staff in 2006. He became the team's head coach during the 2009 season and he was still there in 2020, making him the longest-tenured head coach in league history.

"He's the best leader of an organization in our league, and it's not close," team captain Matt Besler said of his longtime coach in 2019.

BOB GANSLER

Kansas City was stuck at the bottom of the league when Bob Gansler took the reins as head coach in 1999. By the end of the next season, he had helped lead the team all the way to the very top. Gansler was named MLS Coach of the Year in 2000 as his Wizards captured their first MLS Cup. Gansler, who also coached the US men's national team at the 1990 World Cup, stayed with the Wizards until 2006.

Matt Besler played in front of his hometown fans for more than a decade.

HOMETOWN HERO

Vermes proved to be the first of many great defenders to shine for Kansas City. In 2003 Jimmy Conrad began an eight-year run as the Wizards' center back. During that time, the California native scored 17 goals—a team record for a defender—in 204 appearances. He also made the All-Star Game six times and was the 2005 MLS Defender of the Year. Ike Opara won that honor in 2017. Over six seasons with the club, Opara followed Conrad as a force in the central defense.

No Kansas City defender had quite the stature of Besler, though. Besler grew up in Kansas City, watching the Wizards win from the red seats of Arrowhead Stadium. When he grew up, the defender became the team's longtime captain.

Besler was the hometown hero who helped his team reach new heights. He led Sporting to an MLS championship and three US Open Cups alongside a group of talented teammates that included Graham Zusi, Benny Feilhaber, and Kei Kamara.

"I don't want to let them down," Besler told the *Kansas City Star* about his hometown fans. "I feel connected to the people here, to the city, to my friends and family."

Kansas City drafted Besler eighth overall in 2009 out of the University of Notre Dame. The central defender made an impact right away. He made 28 appearances his rookie season and was soon a fixture in the team's backline.

Before long Besler had taken his place among the best defenders in MLS. He was named Sporting's defender of the year four times and took home the MLS Defender of the Year Award in 2012. He made a mark in international soccer, too, with more than 40 appearances for the US men's national team.

Through 2020 Besler made 348 appearances for Sporting. That made him the team's all-time leader in games, starts, and minutes played. However, the team decided not to re-sign Besler after the season, and he moved on to expansion team Austin FC.

THE CAULDRON

Sporting's strengths aren't just on the field. Its fans pack Children's Mercy Park and make it an intimidating place to play. Backing Besler and SKC is one of the loudest groups of fans in MLS. The team's passionate supporters' group is made up of fans who bring the noise for 90 minutes each game.

Soccer supporters are some of the most passionate fans in sports. They stand throughout the game to sing and chant in support of their team. They often wave flags and scarves as they cheer on their favorite players. Their antics make soccer games unlike other sports.

Supporters in the Cauldron make every Sporting KC match a memorable event.

Sporting KC's supporters' group is known as the Cauldron. Two thousand of the team's most passionate fans stand behind the goal in the north end of the stadium each game. They drum, chant, and sing the entire game. It makes for an exciting place to play and can help energize Kansas City's players during tough games.

CHAPTER 4

MEMORABLE MOMENTS

One by one, the pieces came together for Kansas City leading up to the 2000 season. The club featured talented goal-scorers in Preki, Chris Klein, and Chris Henderson. Goalkeeper Tony Meola was one of the best in the league. Then the Wizards added two more key players for the 2000 season. Miklos Molnar, a striker, arrived from Denmark. Veteran defender Peter Vermes, meanwhile, arrived from the Colorado Rapids.

Molnar's lone MLS season was a dream. In 24 league and playoff games, he scored 17 goals. Nine of them were game-winners. Vermes, on the other hand, was the key in a dominant defense. With him and Meola leading the way, no team allowed fewer goals that season.

Sporting Kansas City's Matt McKeon, right, fights off Piotr Nowak of the Chicago Fire in the 2000 MLS Cup.

Miklos Molnar celebrates his goal in the 2000 MLS Cup.

Kansas City's formula paid off in its MLS Cup meeting against the Chicago Fire. The teams took the field on a sunny October afternoon before more than 39,000 fans in Washington, DC. Before long, the Wizards had capitalized on a Chicago mistake and were racing up the field in a lightning-quick counterattack.

Midfielder Klein stormed up the sideline, eluding tackles from Chicago defenders. He played a low, hard pass in front of the Fire's goal. There, Molnar rolled a soft shot past the goalkeeper for a 1–0 lead. After just 11 minutes of their first championship game, the Wizards were on top.

For Molnar, also known as "The Danish Dynamite," the goal was his fifth of the playoffs. It was all the scoring Kansas City could manage that afternoon. But it was enough.

Meola was named the 2000 MLS MVP and Goalkeeper of the Year. And with the league title on the line, he showed why. Meola was unbeatable. Facing a barrage of Chicago shots, the goalkeeper let nothing get past him. His 10 saves included three stops in the final minutes of the game to preserve the Wizards' lead. Meola earned the game's MVP award. With the Supporters' Shield and MLS Cup trophies, the Wizards completed one of the best seasons in league history.

NEW NAME, NEW STADIUM

When Robb Heineman bought the Wizards in 2006, he knew the team was in need of a makeover. The process took time. There were growing pains, too, as the team played temporarily in a minor league baseball stadium. By 2011, though, the team was ready for a fresh start.

Sporting KC's Graham Zusi, *left*, battles David Beckham of the Los Angeles Galaxy in a 2011 match.

The team known for 15 years as the Kansas City Wiz or Wizards changed its name to Sporting Kansas City. The name was a nod to some European clubs that feature teams playing multiple sports. For Kansas City, the name represented the goal of being more than just the local soccer team.

In addition to the new name, the team also changed its colors. The rainbow crest from the team's early years was

> ## WIZARDS WOW MANCHESTER UNITED
>
> It may not have counted in the standings. But when Kansas City beat English soccer giants Manchester United in a 2010 exhibition game, Wizards fans went wild. A record Kansas City crowd of 52,424 at Arrowhead Stadium watched the Wizards shock their guests from England in a 2–1 upset.

long gone. Now the team changed from blue and white uniforms to light blue, indigo, and gray.

For fans, the biggest change came in the form of a new home. After years of playing in stadiums designed for other sports, the Wizards finally got their own $200 million soccer-specific stadium in the suburbs. The stadium, now known as Children's Mercy Park, helped change the atmosphere at Sporting Kansas City games. Empty seats are hard to find. Noisy crowds were now right on top of the action.

Before the new name and stadium, Sporting KC had struggled to draw many fans to games or sell much team merchandise like jerseys and scarves. Kansas City averaged the lowest attendance in MLS nine times in the league's first 14 seasons.

Sporting Kansas City fans now flocked to the new stadium and helped set team attendance records. It didn't hurt that

Kei Kamara converts a penalty kick against Seattle in the 2012 US Open Cup final.

the team also started racking up wins. For a club that had not made the playoffs since 2008, that may have been the most important thing. Kansas City had a new name, a new home, and soon a new position back atop MLS.

SPORTING'S FINEST SPELL

Kansas City settled into its new stadium in 2011. Then Sporting took the league by storm. That season marked the beginning of eight consecutive trips to the playoffs and a haul of trophies to decorate their new home.

The first new addition to the team's trophy cabinet came in 2012. Eight years after their US Open Cup triumph in 2004, Sporting KC fought their way back to that tournament's final. Before a wild Kansas City crowd, Kei Kamara converted a penalty kick with just six minutes to play. That seemed to have clinched the win over three-time defending champion Seattle Sounders. But a Seattle goal just two minutes later sent the game to extra time.

Thirty minutes of scoreless extra time meant Kansas City's US Open Cup fate would be decided on penalty kicks. Both teams converted two of their first four kicks. Sporting's Brazilian midfielder Paulo Nagamura stepped up with the shootout tied at two. He shook off the exhaustion and netted his penalty kick. Jimmy Nielsen saved Seattle's fifth and final attempt to secure the cup. It was a preview of what was to come.

In the 2013 Eastern Conference championship, a talented Sporting side broke a string of bad results in the MLS playoffs. Kansas City advanced all the way to the MLS Cup at home against Real Salt Lake. French defender Aurélien Collin scored for Kansas City late in the second half. But the teams remained tied through regulation and extra time. That brought another dramatic shootout. It went to 10 rounds before the Salt Lake shooter hit the crossbar to give Kansas City its second MLS Cup.

With a lineup full of stars, Sporting continued to be one of the best teams in the league. Forward Dom Dwyer lit up the scoreboard, setting a team record with 23 goals during the 2014 season. All-Stars Matt Besler and Graham Zusi led the team from defense and midfield, respectively. Both were also key parts of the US men's national team at the 2014 World Cup in Brazil.

Sporting followed their second league championship with a third US Open Cup in 2015. Once again, it took another penalty shootout to get their hands on the trophy. Two years later, Kansas City captured another US Open Cup in 2017, its third in six seasons.

Another playoff appearance in 2018 capped the fourth-longest streak of postseason appearances in MLS history. It was one of the most successful stretches in the history of the league. Though the streak was snapped in 2019, Sporting Kansas City turned things around right away, posting the best record in the Western Conference in 2020. Once again, Sporting proved it belongs in the conversation of MLS' best teams.

Dom Dwyer, *center*, is congratulated by his teammates after scoring a goal in 2015.

TIMELINE

1996 — Kansas City earns its first victory, defeating the Colorado Rapids 3–0 before 21,141 fans at Arrowhead Stadium on April 13.

1997 — Wizards star Preki is named MLS MVP.

2000 — Kansas City beats the Chicago Fire in the MLS Cup final 1–0 on October 15 to win its first league championship.

2004 — The Wizards top the Chicago Fire 1–0 on September 22 to capture the club's first Lamar Hunt US Open Cup.

2004 — Kansas City makes its second appearance in the MLS Cup. The team loses 3–2 to DC United on November 14.

2010 — The club unveils its new name and logo on November 17, changing to Sporting Kansas City.

2011 — Playing its first match at Sporting Park on June 9, the club ties the Chicago Fire 0–0.

2012 — SKC defeats the Seattle Sounders in a penalty kick shootout on August 8 to win its second US Open Cup.

2013 — On December 7 SKC beats Real Salt Lake in a penalty kick shootout to win the MLS Cup before 21,650 fans at Sporting Park.

2017 — Sporting wins its fourth US Open Cup title with a 2–1 defeat of the New York Red Bulls on September 20.

TEAM FACTS

FIRST SEASON
1996

STADIUMS
Arrowhead Stadium (1995–2007)
CommunityAmerica Ballpark (2008–10)
Sporting Park/Children's Mercy Park (2011–)

MLS CUP TITLES
2000, 2013

US OPEN CUP TITLES
2004, 2012, 2015, 2017

KEY PLAYERS
Davy Arnaud (2002–11)
Matt Besler (2009–20)
Jimmy Conrad (2003–10)
Chris Klein (1998–05)
Tony Meola (1999–2004)
Ike Opara (2013–18)
Preki (1996–2000, 2002–05)
Alan Pulido (2020–)
Peter Vermes (2000–02)
Kerry Zavagnin (2000–08)
Graham Zusi (2009–)

KEY COACHES
Bob Gansler (1999–2006)
Ron Newman (1996–99)
Peter Vermes (2009–)

MLS MOST VALUABLE PLAYER
Preki (1997, 2003)
Tony Meola (2000)

MLS DEFENDER OF THE YEAR
Matt Besler (2012)
Jimmy Conrad (2005)
Ike Opara (2017)
Peter Vermes (2000)

MLS GOALKEEPER OF THE YEAR
Tim Melia (2017)
Tony Meola (2000)
Jimmy Nielsen (2012)

MLS ROOKIE OF THE YEAR
C. J. Sapong (2011)

MLS COMEBACK PLAYER OF THE YEAR
Eddie Johnson (2007)
Chris Klein (2002, 2005)
Tim Melia (2015)
Tony Meola (2000)

MLS COACH OF THE YEAR
Bob Gansler (2000)

GLOSSARY

cavernous
Featuring a large amount of open space.

corner kick
A free kick from the corner of the field near the opponent's goal.

defenders
Players whose main job is to defend their team's goal against the other team's attack.

extra time
Two 15-minute periods added to a game if the score is tied at the end of regulation.

forwards
Also called strikers, the players who play nearest to the opponent's goal.

golden goal
A goal scored in a sudden-death extra time period that ends the match.

midfielders
Players who stay mostly in the middle third of the field and link the defenders with the forwards.

penalty kick
A play in which a shooter faces a goalkeeper alone; it is used to decide tie games or as a result of a foul.

penalty shootout
A tiebreaker used to decide a match after extra time in which teams alternate kicks against the opposing goalkeeper.

supporters' groups
Fan groups that stand and support their team throughout the game by singing, chanting, drumming, and waving flags.

MORE INFORMATION

BOOKS

Gifford, Clive, and Malam, John. *The Complete Book of Soccer*. Buffalo, NY: Firefly Books, 2016.

Marthaler, Jon. *MLS*. Minneapolis, MN: Abdo Publishing, 2020.

Marthaler, Jon. *US Men's Professional Soccer*. Minneapolis, MN: Abdo Publishing, 2019.

ONLINE RESOURCES

To learn more about Sporting Kansas City, please visit **abdobooklinks.com** or scan this QR code. These links are routinely monitored and updated to provide the most current information available.

INDEX

Besler, Matt, 7–8, 22, 29, 31–32, 42

Collin, Aurélien, 8–11, 41
Conrad, Jimmy, 30–31

DeBrito, Iris, 12
Dwyer, Dom, 22, 42

Feilhaber, Benny, 31

Gansler, Bob, 29

Haverty, Joe, 12
Heineman, Robb, 37
Henderson, Chris, 34

Kamara, Kei, 31, 41
Klein, Chris, 24–26, 34, 37
Klopas, Frank, 16

Meola, Tony, 18, 26–29, 34, 37
Molnar, Miklos, 18, 34, 37

Nagamura, Paulo, 41
Nielsen, Jimmy, 11, 41

Opara, Ike, 31

Palmer, Lovel, 11
Preki, 17, 24–26, 34

Saborío, Álvaro, 6
Simutenkov, Igor, 20

Takawira, Vitalis "Digital," 16–17

Vermes, Peter, 8, 18, 22, 29–30, 34

Zusi, Graham, 7–8, 22, 31, 42

ABOUT THE AUTHOR

Jonathan Avise is a Minnesota United and Tottenham Hotspur supporter who lives in Minneapolis.